# STARSHINE & CLAY

Also by Kamilah Aisha Moon

*She Has a Name*

# Starshine  & Clay

# Kamilah Aisha Moon

Four Way Books
Tribeca

Please direct all inquiries to:
Editorial Office
Four Way Books
POB 535, Village Station
New York, NY 10014
www.fourwaybooks.com

Library of Congress Cataloging-in-Publication Data

Names: Moon, Kamilah Aisha, author.
Title: Starshine & clay / Kamilah Aisha Moon.
Other titles: Starshine and clay
Description: New York, NY : Four Way Books, [2017]
Identifiers: LCCN 2017000673 | ISBN 9781935536956 (pbk. : alk. paper)
Classification: LCC PS3563.O5614 A6 2017 | DDC 811/.54--dc23
LC record available at https://lccn.loc.gov/2017000673

This book is manufactured in the United States of America and printed on acid-free paper.
2nd printing, 2017

Four Way Books is a not-for-profit literary press. We are grateful for the assistance
we receive from individual donors, public arts agencies, and private foundations.

This publication is made possible with public funds from the National Endowment for the Arts

and with public funds from the New York State Council on the Arts, a state agency,

and from the Jerome Foundation.

[clmp]

We are a proud member of the Community of Literary Magazines and Presses.

Distributed by University Press of New England
One Court Street, Lebanon, NH 03766

*The title of this book is an homage of deep admiration and respect for the inimitable, truth-telling treasure and light that Lucille Clifton will always be.*

*Dedicated to my beloveds*

# CONTENTS

# EXPLODED STARS

        haunted by
wholeness—
        bright debris sibilant
beneath skin tug-of-warring
        with gravity, we
harvest shine
        from the caves of
mouths & crevices
        of eyes incandescent
as we remember
        the most massive
flares among us,
        detonate inside
each other to hold
        tiny supernovae
in our arms. Crushed
        bodies craving fusion
keep us brimming
        with enough energy
to pass on,
        keep us lit & lying
to ourselves about
        the eventual & sudden
ways we black hole—
        it already happened, it's happening
anyway, to happen soon,
        scattering all that we think
matters so much now
        for another radiant giant to gather
then fling across galaxies
        again—reconstituted

& scorched clean,
      new turmoil begging
from the inside out
      to burn.

# MERCY BEACH

Stony trails of jagged beauty rise
like stretch marks streaking sand-hips.
All the Earth has borne beguiles us
& battered bodies build our acres.

Babes that sleep in hewn rock cradles
learn to bear the hardness coming.
Tough grace forged in tender bones—
may this serve & bless them well.

They grow & break grief into islands
of sun-baked stone submerged in salt
kisses, worn down by the ocean's ardor
relentless as any strong loving.

May they find caresses that abolish pain.
Like Earth, they brandish wounds of gold!

"who is the human in this place,
the thing that is dragged or the dragger?"

—Lucille Clifton

# THE EMPEROR'S DEER

I.

Their noises make you think
they are crying or suffering.
They have learned to bow.
Even the fawns bow, centuries
of bowing
in their blood.

They are not considered wild.
Precious pests litter parks
with dung, take over the roads.
Sweet nuisance worth
saving, thinning these herds
is a last resort—once
a capital offense to spill
their endangered blood.

They are so used to humans, it is scary.

II.

Our cries are heard as noise,
our suffering considered
natural. Native citizens,
we are not free
to roam or deemed sacred
like Japanese bowing deer protected
as messengers of the gods.

Nara, Japan is known for its temples,
shrines to peace.
America is known for its churches,
segregated Sundays.

This is not Nara, Japan.
Hunted, it is always
open season. The sight
of dark skin brings out the wild
in certain human breeds.
Bowing, hands up
or any other gesture of surrender
makes no difference.

They slay our young & leave them
in the streets, expect us to walk away
& wonder, after centuries
why we are not used to this—

grieving masses treated
like waste, filthy herds
thinned at will.

III.

To be clear, this is America
& we are not deer
We are not deer
We are not dear
here

# ANGEL

"Michael Brown, 18, due to be buried on Monday, was no angel [. . .] "
—John Eligon, *New York Times*

But wasn't he?

Archangel namesake
who weeks before saw his fate
etched into thick gray clouds.
Satan chasing, he saw himself
*running into the face of God,*
wings shrapneled
against future flight under
these skies, this moon.

Another one to hit the ground,
leave us reeling before the Rapture
the faithful still believe in.
Coursing the arterial streets
of cities, his ghost leads holy armies
seeking justice with a heartbeat,
some earthbound salvation.

Michael, the spiritual warrior
& the saint, the chosen
& the fallen. Brown
man-child shattered
in a broken promised land.
Junior, the eternal son
of a brutal, perpetual summer.

They would never paint him
prone & sacred
on any chapel's ceiling—his hands
so dark & sable unlike

God's & Adam's hands, though
in the same image &
weaponless.  Yet scrawled
underneath August clouds forever
is the scene his mother
& the world can't erase.

Weeks before, he called his father at 1 a.m.
after his vision, voice trembling.
Dreaming, he tried to remember
if Heaven was anything like this place—
woke up praying that it wouldn't be
upon his return.

# STATEN ISLAND FERRY RIDE

Boarding the boats, we risk
Middle Passage riptides
still rolling in,
badged sharks
in blue.

Today we board to march
for Eric Garner.
Hooked by hysterical
arms, he thrashed
like a caught thing
on the sidewalk.

We roil past Lady Liberty.
Draped in a dingy gown,
her smudged face
stares back.
Weeds grasp
her hem.

# IMAGINE

*after the news of the dead whether or not we*
*knew them we are saying thank you*
—W. S. Merwin

A blanket of fresh snow
makes any neighborhood idyllic.
Dearborn Heights indistinguishable from Baldwin Hills,
South Central even—
until a thawing happens & residents emerge
into the light. But it almost never snows in L.A.,
& snows often in this part of Michigan—
a declining wonderland, a place not to stand out
or be stranded like Renisha was.

Imagine a blonde daughter with a busted car
in a suburb where a brown homeowner
(not taking any chances)
blasts through a locked door first,
checks things out after—
around the clock coverage & the country beside itself
instead of the way it is now,
so quiet like a snowy night
& only the grief of another brown family
around the Christmas tree, recalling
memories of Renisha playing
on the front porch, or catching flakes
as they fall & disappear
on her tongue.

They are left to imagine
what her life might have been.
We are left to imagine the day
it won't require imagination
to care about all of the others.

# SAMARIA RICE, TAMIR'S MOTHER

Can't live here. Can't live upright now. Just here,
he was. Too quiet, nothing bangs the screen door
or needs new shoes, nothing eats my cooking
or does homework at the kitchen table.
The sky closing, my daughter's mind collapsing
like her baby brother on that grass. Can't live

across the street from that gory field, can't look out
of windows just like the windows some idiot
watched Tamir play from, called in the hit. Can't bury
my son while they bury his case, bury justice
in loopholes & months of red tape. Can't bury the cop,
though I have in my mind many times. Can't deal
with walls, doors. Floors that are too damn clean
of 12-year-old sneaker prints. Can't deal with over *there*

& this never being over. The ground howls,
beckons me as his infant cries once did. Footage
loops on & on—Tamir, Eric, Aiyana,
didn't know murder could look like
wrestling, snuffing bugs, or taking out the trash. Can't live

yards from the chalk outline near hopscotch grids.
My ears can't hold the chirping of birds as if
nothing happened. Can't do it! Lord help me, my child
& mind shot. Always gasping, two-second
discharge, bullet-fast oblivion. Police car
hearse-black. Why is my son not worth pause,
Miranda rights or any other protocol, a bad cop's day

in court? Can't have coffee across from the yawning
green mouth swilling his blood or boil eggs aside
that open coffin. Broken hearts bound
by yellow tape. Done living at this address of can't,
of never again, of not sorry for our loss. Forward
feels pointless; let me live the whole truth now
that my family has been shattered. My head

on this homeless shelter pillow is honest—
there's no safe haven I could ever own.

# PERFECT FORM

*North Charleston, SC, 4.4.15*

Walter Scott must have been a track athlete
before serving his country, having children:

his knees were high, elbows bent
at 90 degrees as his arms pumped
close to his sides, back straight & head up
as each foot landed in front of the other,
a majesty in his strides.

So much depends on instinct, ingrained
legacies & American pastimes.
Relays where everyone on the team wins
remain a dream. Olympic arrogance,
black men chased for sport—
heat after heat
of longstanding, savage races
that always finish the same way.

My guess is Mr. Scott ran distances
& sprinted, whatever his life events
required. Years of training & technique
are not forgotten, even at 50. Even after being
tased out of his right mind. Even in peril
the body remembers what it has been
taught (boy), keeping perfect form
during his final dash.

# FELECIA SANDERS'S GRANDDAUGHTER, 5

*Mother Emmanuel AME, Charleston, SC, 6.17.15*

It was so hot & she promised
we could get ice cream on the way home.

I never saw him at Bible study before.

He didn't smile & I didn't want to say hi
because he was a stranger & Mom said
don't talk to strangers, especially men
you don't know but Grandma told me to be nice.

—

There was popping like firecrackers.

I looked up from coloring & saw
his mouth was a line & people were
falling, red blooms on pastor's white shirt.

Grandma grabbed me & we hit the carpet.
"Play dead baby. Play dead." The words hot
& soft in my ear. We lay real still. Face down,
we held our breath a long long time, longer
than I can even count.

I heard "No!" & "Please," calling on the Lord.
Where were you, Jesus? We pray to you
all of the time & this is your house!

*Click-clack*, more pops & screams.

Grandma was on top of me, warm.
Perfume, powder, sweat & smoke
stung my nose. I felt her heart
beating fast, so fast like after I run
but there was no where to run.

# HUNT (1936 -  )


Already well-fed,
they sniff other quarry
to pass the days,
roaming & tracking fear
in fine leather shoes, sneakers,
combat boots.

Back then & now, bloodhounds
walk their dogs,
sic terror at too many turns—

Double-breasted, t-shirted,
uniformed beasts
always on the prowl.

## FIVE

black men

    spun like tops. Temptations

that died in unison

    under Alabama sun,

tangled together on lines

    spooled around the same tree—

fresh catch.

  I wish

    they could've hummed

       to heaven

instead of being hooked      then flung there.

# THE OAK TREE'S BURDEN

To Clyde Johnson, lynched August 3, 1935

*Your weight*
*bows my branch*
*toward the earth*

*I was not made for this*

*I will never be the same*
*Bent*
*like a fractured*
*            unset bone*
*that cannot heal straight*

*Gnarled in eternal nod*
*like your bark-colored head*

*So heavy*
*our body-breaking hour*

*Please*
*forgive me*

# TO JESSE WASHINGTON

I.

A chill shot through
your mother's body
when you did not come home

Breath caught in her throat
when your trachea snapped

The heat baked her
as your skin flaked off
Flames licking you free

II.

One smirked as he leaned
against skinned wood proud
of his charred trophy
Your soul fuming
through smoke

White cloth draped your loins
bright & unsoiled
A skirt across
the sawed-off stub

But nothing could cover
or civilize this somehow
Certain images
do not bury well

III.

Even in death
your fried arms curled up
into the strong man pose

Your bones still rattle
& reek in charbroiled wind

You were not the spectacle

# THE ACCUSED'S LAST STAND

Your gaze lets on
that you were playing chicken
with death in those final moments—
& almost won.

The welts & bruises
swell into instant warrior marks.
(Like Shaka, you knew
they would come.)
More beautiful than Job,
you squint past misery.

Somebody wanted to have your babies.
Children so magnificent,
they wouldn't have survived either—
slaughtered by brimmed men
masking wick-less eyes
insanely jealous
of the flame in yours.

No matter how long the torment,
you would not beg.
Naked but not stripped,
they wasted this kill on you.

# PEELING POTATOES AT TEREZIN
## CONCENTRATION CAMP

Ribbons of skin pile at our feet;
we count wet orbs like heads.
Beneath the blades, white meat.

Their kitchens are not kosher or neat.
The knives engrave our dread.
Ribbons of skin pile at our feet.

They will salt these crops, a doomed fleet
torn from the earth's cold bed.
Beneath the blades, white meat

to be mashed or boiled, a treat
ravished to nothing but shreds.
Ribbons of skin pile at our feet,

flesh carved in dangling sheets—
slice after jagged slice spread
beneath the blades, white meat.

We work under the glare, a street
of eyes gouged & shed.
Ribbons of skin pile at our feet.
Beneath the blades, white meat.

# AFTER RESCUE FROM BOKO HARAM

Schoolgirls, God's crop
raided by rebels
wielding their knives,
guns. Girls shot through
by barreled fury
hanging between heavy
booted legs that crush.

Could any god be pleased?
Tumored hearts, sick thunder
racking dregs of men
infected by "the western plague"
they rage against—there's no monopoly
of any cardinal direction or sin,
just red & more red.

Rotund, gaunt-faced girls
stand on thin legs seeking rations,
back from the hell of Sambisa Forest.
(What is it about making trees
accomplices?) The beating sun
grins, yet one manages the miracle
of a true smile.

In a matter of weeks, babies
shall wail bloody for the murdered,
inconsolable as young scholars
dragged from their desks
into this wretched calculus, infinite
aftermath.

Marauding cowards, leviathan lust
swelling hundreds of pubescent bellies
standing in line waiting as if life
is business as usual because
it is. Godammit it is.

# ETERNAL STAND

*The hand on a statue of Jefferson Davis in the Jefferson Davis Library holds
the confederate flag, blown there by the winds of Katrina, Sept. 12, 2005,
in Biloxi, MS. The historic grounds withstood the strength of Hurricane
Camille in 1969, the worst recorded hurricane to hit the Mississippi Gulf
Coast, but buckled under the strength of Katrina.*
              *—CBS News caption*

Some try to lynch his legacy,
rip what's stitched in the nation's blood.
But Jefferson won't be moved—
a bold, living relic of stone.
Ask the fields, ask the floods.
He refuses to surrender his home.

He spent his breath to keep this home.
Flew the "stars and bars," whose legacy,
long after the war, is buoyed by floods
of praise & staunch, Southern blood.
His heirs picked a slab of stone
to chisel legs that won't be moved.

His rebel heart has never moved,
grounded firmly in the dust of home.
Dark rain dries on cheeks of stone,
warmed in the sun of this land's legacy.
His shriveled veins, clear of blood,
yet nothing—not the vast floods

   of Camille, or the fresh floods
   of Katrina—washes his legacy
   hell-bent on not being moved.
   Yes, even evil needs a home
   where roses bloom bright as blood,
   frame front porches made of stone.

God can't rinse the sneer from stone,
as the gulf fills with blood.
Rivers rage through his home,
papers & books lost to the floods
but the history won't be moved—
hurricanes too weak for this legacy.

Presidents bow to his legacy;
prejudice bequeathed by blood.
Rescue squads won't be moved
to save bodies swollen stiff as stone.
Spirits ferried by the floods
to heaven, a kinder, gentler home.

Jefferson's home ravaged by floods,
but his beloved legacy hasn't moved.
His stone hand clutches a flag, red as blood.

# SHARED PLIGHT

Bound to whims,
bred solely for
circuses of desire.
To hell with savannahs,
towns like Rosewood.

Domestics or domesticated,
one name or surnamed, creatures
the dominant ones can't live without
would truly flourish
without such devious love,
golden corrals.

Harnessed. Muzzled.
Stocks & bonds. Chains
& whips held by hand.
Ota Benga in a Bronx cage,
Saartjie Baartman on display—
funds sent to her village
didn't make it okay.  Harambe,
Tamir, Cecil, Freddie—names
of the hunted, captives
bleed together. The captors
beasts to all but themselves
& their own.

Two endangered beings in a moat
stare into each other's eyes.

Slower than light, mercy
must not survive entry
into our atmosphere, never
reaching those who lose
unbridled lives
long before they die
in this world of zoos
& conquerors who treat
earthlings like aliens.

"Make of my anguish / more than I can make. Lord, hear my prayer."

–Christian Wiman

# TO THÉMA, ALMOST TWO YEARS AFTER
## YOUR BURIAL

I don't know their names
& they don't know yours,
though your flesh is now
of their flesh as a donor.

I try not to get angry
at strangers pressing too close,
choosing kindness just in case
there's a part of you
brushing by.  What have
your gorgeous, castaway eyes
gifted another to see?
I must have dined near what remains
of you, faithful organ
thriving in a body
spending your hours, strolling past
milestones you won't reach.     Your children

play around us, your laugh
inside tiny throats, holding their bodies
the way you held yours
against fading light, letting music enter
& move them alive. Alive!  Your name
sweet pepper burning your parents' tongues,
the spice of you fresh as the day
they brought you home.

In lieu of flowers, this. Oh cousin,
you know the deepest sacrifice—
being a miracle is far from the glory
of receiving one. No longer blessed,
you live on as blessing.

# STILL LIFE AS ROCKET: 42

*Thanks, Yolonda*

This is the part where the boosters begin
to fall away, & I'm moving so fast
it feels like slow motion.
From here I can see
the blue contours of my journey
against eternal midnight lit
with torches held by unseen hands.
I understand why many choose
not to look—it really does take
my breath away, steers this ride toward
terror & away from thrill. I think of
Joy, Théma, Kerry, Anthony, Phebus. Sandra & those
lynched by cops, satellite spirits
who didn't reach this orbit alive, how I must
feel the fuel burning & praise them
by not cursing the mirror or clinging
to the rear view & its new
blurriness; dare to comb defiant curls
emblazoned by moonlight.
There is so much still launching
in me.

# COUP IN PROGRESS

The vultures land & land,
dark-bodied vigils on the train tracks,
striding across bald front yards, alighting
on chipped, white steeples.

The wait is just about over, the breath
of intervention ragged.
Feasting on decaying neighborhoods
that fringe cities with resurrected
midtowns, they scout
the next meal. Apparently here

is next—where we learned to pedal, then drive
up & down these hilly streets, where parents lay
their gray heads. Vultures, almost
grinning, spread night-hued wings
across this overcast, blank afternoon
between Christmas & New Year's Eve,
living as they do to steal the scraps
between endings & beginnings.

A daughter home for the holidays, the whiff
of death beneath pine-scented candles,
on the heels of baked goods & bleach,
wafting from dingy storefronts
& a rancid creek that once teemed
with crayfish, children holding hands to not slip
on mossy stones in summer.

The everyday residents can't tell me
how long the clawed ones have been coming around
surveying, cawing to each other,
*soon*. Vultures, flaunting
their haughty asses in our faces.
No one names the vultures
in suits holding offices, the bottom feeders
at the top. No one reclaims
this brink, beaks & bullies multiplying.

# THE FIRST TIME I SAW MY MOTHER WITHOUT
# HER PROSTHESIS

*after Hafizah Geter*

Like the smooth face of the cliff
she was just thrown from, the left
side of her chest was flat
& blank, save for two tiny
raised scythes. Not a half-carved
turkey, thankless,
but a woman.


It almost seemed as if her breast
could be drawn back on again,
as if the scalpel was merely
erasing cancer, as if the right one
hanging like a luminous brown
tear wasn't the lonely twin.
As if this new lightness
didn't threaten to render her
a widow of his touch,
de-mother her somehow.

Is this a crystal ball moment—
the fanged, wily shadow
never outrun or outwitted?


—

*Do you want to see, baby?*


I couldn't say no—her love
never flinched, neither would I.

# OVERHEARD ON BEDFORD AVENUE

You deliver a sermon in the street.
27 degrees, hollering at everyone
& no one about workers' rights.

If you worked a first shift, you would be winding
down, 10 minutes until clocking out. If.

Reciting from a crumpled pamphlet,
your nose runs, but you carry on as if
this doesn't matter, just like it doesn't matter
if only the manholes & the rats teeming below
hear your twilight tirade.

The plastic bags rustle in the trash cans
& the filthy snow knows
what those hours cost you.

I see your pink, swollen face. I see
a dad dismissed after 36 ripe years
without fruit for his silver days.

You wade into streams of cars proselytizing,
brave the wind's whips & lashes, stop
just short of squealing.

Already ran over, look at your house
of bones & skin, blown. The wolves
are winning.

# CATARACTS

When life scuffs & finally scars the eyes
they become turtles—withdraw inside themselves,

dive inside private marshes, dragging under
the once-girl they belong to, the dewy woman

who rolled them in pleasure, then cried her children
here, blinking back. They retreat into hardness,

she squints at every wound. After all, why this cruel
gauze now? Over 66 years of scenery, fate's

scattershot survived thus far—have they seen enough,
growing armor that only a highly-skilled violence

can remove? She goes under, begs the rest—
tissue, organs, & membrane to please hold on,

still eager to behold (until that final haze)
some sliver of disheveled beauty. The eyes

of her dreams carapace, zig-zag & buzz trapped
inside latched windows. There is no surgery for this.

# INITIATION

*for Rachel Eliza*

Your friend has entered the tribe
of those who've buried their mothers
& she is different—more of herself
than ever, but a new layer, the affect
of one unable to shake the sounds
of leaving, to unsee profound rising
preceding her own, waiting. *What day
is it, does it matter? Where am I,
the keys?* Inducted into a society
of hurried truces & anointing
that becomes a steady hum
in the music of all things.

The full, gray sky held its water
as she rained & rained, a rain
that will never dissipate, her legs
forgetting for a spell why they were made,
her husband's arms remembering
what they're for. Shining, gorgeous grief—
death's anchor a terrible salvation to a family
adrift. The sob & tremble of *gone,
gone* coursing through clasped hands.

The duty of firstborn daughters,
how it lengthens the spine & hollows
the cheeks as she holds the widower's hand.
Her crowded face in the mirror,
morning walks with the "grand-dog"
ambushed by epiphany (oh, the babies
she won't meet!) At any hour, snippets
of speech, sensation & memory surge—

stranding former selves as starfish & conchs
strewn on some remote beach. The thought
of calling, of being called stopped
in its tracks    *No—the ground opened*
*& we gave her back,*
*shut down the interstate &*
*stood without falling among*
*all of those stones.*

When mothers are lowered, daughters
break out of boxes, unbossed by
the minutia that comes with breathing.
You saw it happen, see it in your friend's
furrowed brow, the revised way she leans
in a doorway, across a kitchen counter.

Her mother has gone there, dragging her
into a new here. This missing flares. Gone
is the banter of carefree homegirls;
a deeper cadence reigns—that grown alto, *mama*
heavy on her tongue, loud & loving
in her mind, in lucid dreams.
Heiress to her mother's wellspring & might,
she finally gets what *hmph* really means.

When mothers are planted,
daughters begin a furious blooming.

# FIBROIDS

## I.

Women carry
rogue galaxies
Ultrasound reveals
bitter planets spinning
beneath navels
A twining of all
we've been forced
to ingest

## II.

We sail grimaced & slow
with unwanted cargo
through Bermuda
triangles of blood

## III.

Sour seeds, viscous
evidence of giving Trouble
the once over, still offering
a warm bed. Or proof
of having done nothing
nothing at all

## IV.

Strange plums, melons tumble
& break over themselves,

leaving little room
for a child's head—
siphoning until lungs
beat & the heart
gasps

# TRANSFUSIONS

I've bled too much
& the little blood left
doesn't know what to do
with itself.

My lengthy stint as a dismissed
unsolved puzzle ends
with a crime scene cab ride,
crimson shoeprints in snow.

Two men—a brawny, West Indian nurse
& an intern with a Sinatra smile, listen
to my sallow skin & sunken eyes,
the gasp of my organs finally
audible to ears
human enough to hear.

How does blood forget itself?
What made amnesia better
than remembering?
Un-mined ore, my soul's wildlife
slick & gagging.

The white coats
who never talk to each other
& only talk at me say
an essential hardness is absent,
leaving me an unlocked
bar-less window in a

depressed neighborhood.
But the IV of pure iron
brings torrents of sweat,
shuts throat & half-nelsons
lungs to knees. See,

I am soft—
tissue, tendons, & tears.
Use what I am
to heal me. Type for type,
a universal donor
needs her own kind
for support unlike
an electric charge
fueled by opposites,
that stunning danger.

These bright hanging
bags, this tube
a charming snake
I don't know (Eve's tripwire?).
The line glows red
& I pray this gift
is a kind cure:
crushed violets trellis
my arms, sites
of puncture & exit
so sore I won't settle
for anemias of any sort again.

Despite past blunders,
the reddest of fears, I hope
to have bold faith in a stranger's
generous body again.

# AFTER SURGERY: RESCUE

Binding me in white,
a cacophony of hands drag me
from drugged oblivion—
*Wake up, we're done,*
*you made it through.*

The last thing I remember
is a nurse humming, stroking
my temples like a girlfriend
behind the paper mask.

As light flooded back in,
the second thing I see
is my father's smiling face
ready to feed me ice chips.

Did he stare at me this way
the first time I emerged
swaddled through swinging doors?
How loved am I; though no longer
new, less & less beautiful.

*You made it through*, they said.
My father's eyes confirmed.
But now what—

plumbing fixed, womb
rebuilding itself (show the rest
of me how, please),
will I make sure this rescue
isn't in vain, rising
from the table healing
or merely patched?

# AFTER SURGERY: INVASIVE

The almost, unsound sleep.
Fluorescent, beeping nights & drab,
venetian-slatted days
of nurse shifts—
crapshoot of care. No thanks,
I'll insert the suppository
my damn self & take
back the pneumonia,
please, such promiscuous
hands

& the green interns
playing doctor on the
live broken doll
with my drawn eyes.
Rounds of them gawk
& handle,
unsheathed fingers
not asking consent.

As if I am amphibian
& straight-pinned
to this awful bed.
As if I am not threatened
by fever.
As if my soft, barely
insured octaves
don't count.

That's it—the slither
of my eyebrow
freezes them, hisses
*Enough.*

# AFTER SURGERY: SCAR

The pink
glossy planaria
sewn

into the sandy flesh
of my abdomen
hovers above a portal—

what I feared might
divide
has only doubled
my powers

# AFTER SURGERY: RIDING IN MY BODY
## WITH OTHERS IN THEIRS

All afternoon I pleased myself.
To hell with work, I needed to know
that I still work, pleasure
still possible. My body able to say
*yes* after trauma, sigh into itself
without deep revolt, passion
without reprisal. Took matters
into my own smooth, hungry hands.
Praise God I have some control;
the saving grace of a room
in a rented apartment,
the shield of a plywood door.

\*


The old woman did not have that same grace
tonight, subway car bench
turned bed. Our commuter eyes
bays that her robust wave of urine
rushed toward, cascading across the long seat—
a putrid falls that doused bags & feet
not fast enough to move in time.

We scrambled as if it were acid.
Aghast, anxious laughter & the rueful
shaking of heads as if we knew
something about being human
that she didn't.

What could she do but slump
into damp, uneasy slumber?
Everyone rattling along, jerking

with each start & stop—
the involuntary, inevitable tributaries
splitting off to chase
each of us down.

# PRODIGAL DAUGHTER

I've come to keep the fallings at bay.
But listen, this NY parish doesn't sing gospel
the right way. They don't *sang* it—
leaving out shouts, moans, vocal runs
& downhome syntax—"I just can't give up now"

will never be "I don't feel no ways tired."
Not the same! I can hear the notes
missing how the old words fit. This is not
the song I need to sing tonight. How foolish,
attempting to properly conjugate struggle.

Who proclaimed the healing mojo
of wood altars, blood-red carpets, & stained glass?
A single cross hanging; polished brass bowls.
It must be real, found all over the world
configured like this & me, bowing before it,
finally understanding what *beseech* really means.

Lines form to pray & wash hands.
About to sprinkle my face, the last thought
I should be thinking stops me. Who knows
where all of these hands have been!
& could my clean be someone else's filth?
How silly to be on this earth nearly 40 years
& still worry about contamination. Everything
has been touched, even what was

buried in ice, thawing again. The subway full
of sin, the sullied riding side by side. Seems like
my feet used to peel & remain soft on their own.

But when I look down now, heels hardened by all
they've had to carry, or stare at what happened
to my face after an unholy baptism,
no amount of scrubbing matters.

I've come to be saved, to remember why
I'm still worthy. But I'm becoming convinced
a good memory is a passport to hell.
Perhaps like those in Manila & the Gulf Coast,
I want water to be a good thing again,
like love. How strange to answer the begging
of so many thirsts, unable to swallow.

# MADEAR TESTS POSITIVE

Logger of long hours inside
& outside of home,
night-gowned lighthouse,
owner of used breasts, tear-soaked
shoulders & a well-worn lap,

in whose arms
could you have rested,
succumbed without fear
of breaking boughs, hell
or high water to pay
for pleasure, for remembering
you are a woman?

Love dropped you, hard
from over 30 years high.
Who wouldn't take the first
warm, veined hand offered?
How could you have known he was
a sharecropper of loneliness,
sower of radioactive
sweet nothings like seeds,
bathing you in bittersweet brine
without apology or gratitude
before diving his dwindled self
back into the earth?

You couldn't, like none of us could
or can know. Yet, as every other crisis
lived through, you remain royal
in faith-rending circumstances
still, still. & always.

An exhale after waiting
for so long shouldn't cost
this much. When the worst
befalls the best, injustice
stuns us silent as a dying star
weeping alone in the dark sky
to herself.

Queen mother, burn
until your breath
becomes holy smoke.

# HER POEM STUNS MINE INTO HOLDING ITS HEAD

—I asked them to "draw a map" of where they come from. For L's brave
beauty in workshop . . .

*I can only write about the inside,* she says. *Is this ok?*
Where she's from, luxuries include bread, sun, & fresh air.
A shell of Mom tokes against porcelain, writhes away.

A soiled mattress in the corner where she & grandma lay
as rats, bold & satisfied, trespass tangled limbs, bare.
*I can only write about the inside,* she says. *Is this ok*

for cool water to seep through cracks in the hallway,
rivers tasted in the hell of an abandoned, concrete lair
& a shell of Mom tokes against porcelain, writhing away

while weird uncles creep & slither . . . a dropped daughter prays,
stomachs everything but food, looks up & declares
*I can only write about the inside. Is this ok?*

Her eyes, more luminous than bare bulbs, sway
between visions of clean windows & the fried hair
of a Mom's shell toking against porcelain, writhing away

as hunger mauls & love cooks in a dirty pipe. This day,
we listen, nod, cry when she wails "this shit ain't fair!"
*I can only write about the inside. Is this really ok*
to have a shell of Mom toking against porcelain, writhing away?

# FAMILY TIES UNLACED

Went to the Smithsonian Museum of African Art
to feel a connection
Learn some culture
& view ancestral artifacts

My distant kin
from across the water

Feeling instead the chasm of the gift shop
where black cashiers grin & chat
with white customers but turn
into stone figures
while ringing up
my poster
key chain
& bookmark

My distant kin
from across the counter

# RECOVERY

Strange racket shatters my sleep.
Muscles knotted as a rasta's mane,
heart turned scared hummingbird,
I listen longer & finally recognize rain.

Dear God, rain is even suspect now—
eerie percussion in the narrow alley between
stone walk-ups. Trees catch it
so much sweeter; I'm missing years
of soft green landings
in the dead of this night.

My body clenches,
fails to forget. Damn,
not the rain, too.

I smiled & spoke to them every day.
These steel pan-voiced men—
gargoyles perched on the stoop
with laughing red eyes,
have long smoked or drank
what they took while I was at work,
scoping for months until
they knew my darkened
corridors better than I did.

How do I file what has happened?
Hope they are haunted
by the hard drive
of my exquisite music,
digital images of a man

who loves the daughter
they ransacked. I weep for
the first lines of a novel learning
to stand on its own, lost.

Oh, the excruciating xylophone
of rain pelting new iron bars.
It sounds like a window gate

screeching open, a rug flipped over,
a lock fiddled with. A fractured,
incessant gutter song.

# ANOTHER EPISODE IN THE CITY

A rickety man at Burger King
talks & laughs to himself.
Scarecrow of concrete, he pops
out of his seat like a jack-in-the-box;
performs a kind of urban tai chi, drool
a pendulum from his lips. I wonder
what music moves him into sweet
oblivion, renders him
a blessed stowaway
from this dingy day's madness—

snatching bliss like street kids
who only get relief from the heat
when there is a loosening or break
in the main.

# SELF-PORTRAIT AS A BODEGA IN SUNSET PARK

I am the tight aisles & crammed shelves
stocked with a dusty surplus of goods
waiting to expire,
watching the people come & go.

I am the Tecate tallboy Felipe plunks
his buck-fifty down for every day.

I am the cat, rubbing up against everything;
the batteries, incense, & candy behind
the counter & the "EBT now accepted here" sign.

I am the wrinkled biddy jumping everyone in line
asking twenty questions; the chubby kid
begging for an Italian ice, any cheap sweetness.

I am the cigarette smoke just outside the door; the Arab brothers
who've been here for years & the cousin who just arrived
last month, hitting on everything that moves & sleeping on the floor.

I am the mom who opens, the pop who stays until 9 p.m.
& the son who closes, bachata music blaring.

I am the salt-&-pepper-haired woman they can't peg.
Sounds & dresses like a professor, buys beer
like a coed. Looks Dominican yet speaks no Spanish.

I am the smeared glass face of the tiny deli—
the sourdough hardening in trapped air.

At some point, I became a front for something else.
Both fixture & farce of the corner, a way station
in ceaseless traffic.

# TORRENT

On a night among hacking hangers-on
snaking through the bowels of three boroughs
haunted by millions of hungers,
how to coax poems & brightness
beyond bars at Rikers—ward off
darkness that isn't true love
or kin? What to make of this
mildewed night
where nothing sates, the bad batch
of everything
comes to your table?
Tonight feels like a hazing
as heavy rain batters
cheeks stained
into relief maps of regret.
A black-eyed van with a bum muffler
barrels past, barely missing you
but all you notice is rain—
you, a blues groan, blur
of woman washed down
slick, empty blocks as gutters
gag on golden leaves.

# SONG OF SOLOMON REMIX

If a child already burdened
by his tombstone name ventured off
the beaten path into backwoods
to peer into the windows of my life
he would see little, thus seeing
way too much. My kitchen
has no pulse, my pots not slick
from use. I don't shuck anything.

He would see one woman, face unmade
& breasts exposed, dressing for the day
from a heap on the floor, or dozing upright
in a cracked, fifth-hand chair. Blankets
twisted in sweat & serrated sunlight—
scenes of quiet disaster seared
into tiny retinas. No harmonies
riding breezes to bring comfort or joy.

When did the need for nourishment flip
into a desperate feeding of desire?
This figment of boy hunched in the shadows
yearns for the broken chains
of parents' choices chapter & verse
to give him something to strive for!
Who wants to be born unable
to outrun blue-lipped destiny?

I yearn to cut my matted hair
so a woman's hands will run through it
to make me over.
The last woman's hands lost

in my thick roots unraveled me,
sparked a prolonged fever.

Less magic than mayhem beneath
my navel (I'm no Pilate or angel),
I've lived long enough to know
why a man would choose a moment
of soaring over a train of unsung years
freighted with loss & memory.

I don't wish this knowing
on anyone's child—
especially a son's soul growing among trees
that might be watching.

"because the ground won't thaw,
no matter how we press skin
to skin,                    make a fire from
this friction we call love."

—Jehanne Dubrow

# #1

Oh, we turn & turn
& often, breathlessly, click
but never open

# WISH

"Es tan corto el amor, y es tan largo el olvido."
(Love is so short, and forgetting is so long).
—Pablo Neruda


I could bypass & reverse heartbreak
back to when we stood on a busy subway platform,
a pair of brown, ripe pear trees parting brooks
of people. We leaned in for a kiss
that fluttered like a million monarchs
landing at once. We were striking like giraffes
transported from the bed we'd just made into
a private starry savannah in Harlem, taller
& more beautiful than anything else. I began
to grow another chamber that summer afternoon
after your birthday, just for you.

Or to Love Fountain in Philly, the wet reaching
skyward, a series of risings like us
night after night, eventually falling back into, then away
from each other. The mist, our braided fingers,
your Indian profile, the green bench that held
a shimmering, shared peace.

Somewhere inside the pale rose
of that deep chamber, I'm still sitting there
with the you who loved me
even as my coin rusts among other hopes
at the bottom of a shallow pool in a city
where neither of us live.

# DEAR GOD PLEASE MAKE ME A BIRD

would i be a blue heron, or a sparrow?
what's it like to be you, chickadee?
something ferried by the wind
for miles with little effort—an eagle
of crannies, refugee of nooks, wingspan
more than enough
for your body. sometimes, being in this body

dealing with other bodies is too much. orioles
are nice, orange stripes gleaming. no more
miles of arteries to feed. everything measured
in swift, sure beats. heart flutter, blackbird wings
in the sweet pit of her when we made love. better
than trudging uphill alone, lying face down inside.
who wants that? folks live & leave life that way
all the time.    now dying mid-flight—
that's something to pray for.    a crane, whooping?

# #17

How long will you lay there,
heaping days lodged
beneath your mourning,
sheets bearing only
your scent?

Your heart has grown rough
stubble, heartbreak's porcupine
piercing all that is good
surrounding it.

Be brave again, don't stay
in shambles.
You fashioned a goddess
but she was never worth
immortal misery. Who is?

How long will you sleep
until it hurts, the bed
shoving back? Eyes, everything
willed shut, the birds singing
for their own sake.

# A GOLDEN SHOVEL

Bright fields recede to jigsaw pieces as the
plane tugs us closer to heaven, the grasses
uniform from this view, none of us forgetting
how hunger & thirst chain bodies to their
demands. Oh, how to ignite a soul blaze
that doesn't require sustained burning &
ash clearing, the caresses of two consenting
adults to sanction an impossible ceremony—to
bless the searing green of it all, & the brown.

The wrong ghost beckons me by name to come:
she wants me to lean into arms that aren't there,
to find solace in thin air. Que sera sera, what shall
be shall be. Damn, so much woman unable to be
solid or certain in any way, earth-toned skin such
a ruse. Despite a continent of memories, islanding
those misspent years proves brutal to recover from,
winnowing wisdom from stubborn grains of grief.

# ALLERGY (WHY WE CAN'T BE FRIENDS)

From the residue, love remains
strewn through everything. Our dander
taxes all of my passages.
What we hold close can choke us.

Strewn through everything, our dander
trips beautiful memory, a fallen thing.
What we hold close can choke us,
make it difficult to breathe.

Trips . . . beautiful memory a fallen thing
not worth revisiting. To keep coming here
makes it difficult to breathe—
what's gone pervades this air anyway.

Not worth revisiting, to keep coming here
stings—demise has spoken.
What's gone pervades this air anyway;
the best relief is total retreat.

Stinging, demise has spoken—
taxing all of my passages!
The best relief is total retreat
from the residue of love remains.

# EX-CROSSING

A moment dreaded
for years turns out to be
pedestrian—something that once flew
grounded. On a lit Manhattan
corner, there's a nip in the late April wind—
last season's long, graceless goodbye
& both of us wrapped up in it.

You lean against the storefront
a strange, ghosted beauty,
my lovely scald branding
someone else's skin. Split-second
reaction, I walk by, then walk back
a few steps just to be sure
& to let you witness me
seeing you in context, finally—
bright promise horizoned, swoon
without waiting arms, my heart's
swan dive into an empty pool.

I wave & mean it both ways.

The fool in me still moths to your flame,
but the fresh silver in my hair
streaks past the nightclub throbbing
with music & friends we love
where I know you are going, steers
ruby-canvased, Hermes-swift feet

around one corner, then another.

# THESE ARE THE BREAKS

Oh broken bewildered girl I wasn't born to be, break
yesterday under heel. With each step I won't break

apart like old cake on a cracked plate
deserted, the fate of wasted sweetness, or break

like a dropped heart's smithereens
speckling sand until fresh waves break

over, wash them into crowded sea. Bruised
moon drawn to gritty, slick earth, break

her pull, resume rightful orbit
in the vast, vast sky—never should a break

up break life in two. Ever. No one
but Christ with His Before & After can break

time's body like that, shock dark hair white
with belief. This is my story, my song—let me break

it down: I'll glow with *borrowed splendor*, ripen
my soul day & night between clouds, break-

through wide & undeniable, fuse a new Aisha
with what remains, resists & refuses to break.

# UMPTEENTH CODA

My body was too much
like your body, the contrasts
recalling girls you envied
& hated in school. My former
cloud of hair, my skirts
& blouses, my breasts
wrecking balls to the swagger
you craved. I caved
to keep us, you bulldozed
the rest. Facing your chosen
choir, you kept your back to me
& never had mine. We didn't have
a chance. Hapless pilgrim
intoning your name (except
for that one, awful time after days
without sleep), my devoted
tongue roamed you, ringing.

You didn't warn me until too late—
taught me sex
as vengeance, all bow
& no violin (Neglect christens
any friction or sound music).
You doubled every thirst

yet I kept singing *come by here*
as if you were my lord, able
to fix a broken savior.          Marred,
wet months wheeled into misshapen
years spinning at the wrong speed,
drying into a clusterfuck

of wrongs glazed over.        I know
the exact moments when I became
everyone else to you.        How I pay
& pay—you didn't warn me
so now I live with nothing
can be done.

Your grown, lived-in body rife
with radiant scars I adore
houses the heart of a toddler full of *gimme,*
*all mine* & *no!* I chose to mother
that heart, chase after a love wired
to depart. I ran out of everything,
stopped because I had to.

As if you were my friend, I asked
for joint absolution, closure.
But you prefer me limbo'd
in loss, barely breathing
in your memories cinched
& quiet as theory—once again
left on my own to find release.
You never could handle me
embodied; I must houdini
funk into sanctified blues!

Even so, how we spooned is a holiness
that existed, fleeting sublime
that craters. Heart-rain, please end
for the people we could have
never been to each other.

# ONE REASON WHY PARTS OF SPEECH MATTER

From far away in a new bed
she told me I was "a treasure"
& it slapped harder
than an epithet. Not another,
not again—
I cannot bear it.

—

You, the beautiful blur on the hill
smiling & gazing directly
with the sweet, hooded eyes of love:
when we finally reach each other,
don't say anything—just *treasure* me

instead of calling me one
as you bury me in the dirt
of a past only valuable
to pirates, paupers
& explorers who come
after

"Music of hair,
 Music of pain,
 music of looms weaving all our loves again."

—Galway Kinnell

# LOVE

Once you've decided (it is a decision)
your skull won't bleach
in the sun like a lost animal, what else
is there to do in any desert but study at the feet
of succulents drawing relief out of no where,
bristle with lessons? To walk & walk far past
whatever singed—the trudge
of faith every body afire knows until some
inexplicable, glorious flower or face
sirens the water & honey rooted in your cells, rolls
all of the little stones away from the tomb
that still is your heart & roars
without words, *rise*

# A NEW NOVA SPEAKS

For Cain, Jehan . . .


No longer a little boy
I am light again
Spectacular & pure
Brilliant silver glow
above your creased foreheads

Do not unravel
Chase blame or curse the moon
Face the sable sky each night
Sing us all to sleep

I am light again
My arms reach from heaven
Rays of love streaming
through your dreams

Let the rain cease
Make new wishes
Bask in my shine
Inherit me as hope

I blaze in all of you

# GOOSE-DAUGHTER LAMENT

This bird with 99 heartbeats soars
into purple sky seeping
through the last orange streak of day.

Gliding back & forth across seasons
to my flock, I sit buckled by the movement
that happens between visits. The displacement
of frosted hairlines, the keys
that become harder to find.
Furniture discarded after years
of couching sweet struggles,
dream-stained cushions lying in a dumpster.
Vinyl records & soft-spine novels wink
like long-ago friends. There's less & less
space for things acquired outside
of these maturing walls. But a corner
of room left doesn't matter

as we cluster like Mama's wedding ring.
She presses gold into my palm this time,
a talisman. Or perhaps a compass to guide me
through this next stretch of woman turbulence.

# HOLIDAY DETOUR THROUGH LONG HUNTER
STATE PARK

The wide, obsidian eyes
of does, bucks, & fawns
target us huddled lakeside
snapping sister-selfies to record
our great fortune: we're all
still here. More & less
of who we were when
we arrived one after the other,
then another.

This isn't the usual way
to our parents' house,
but something in my sister urges
*keep driving, follow this road*
*wherever it goes.* It doesn't
lead us back like she thought it would—
home isn't the compass
it once was.

Not lost, we get out to survey
bare trees that dwarf us—
spark charcoal memories, the din
of high-pitched squeals as we
dashed these trails during picnics
summers ago. We wonder
how the mallards & deer feel
about December, how we feel
bundled in wool & holding onto each other
as the wind picks up,
things changing by degrees.

Naked, horned
unblinking life surrounds us;
sunset caws begin.
We look up, at least for now
we have this vast, sherbert sky
& a bridge to cross
above chilly waters.

# BOWLING ON THURSDAYS

Tear-filled eyes peer
through Marlboro haze to see
jumbo jawbreakers careen
toward defenseless pins

With each triumph & near-triumph
a barrage of accolades & high-fives follow
Each release fueled by stress & monotony
The best lauded
The worst teased then consoled
Everyone laughs at bad puns

No talk of the economy
war or police brutality
Not a word about Sophie's
13-year-old pregnant daughter
or Craig's failure to show up
most of the time
Just tired regular folk pausing
from a fast-forward life
Assembled to guzzle Michelob
& wait their turn

# WHAT THE OLD ROSES SAID

These roses have gone down well.
Blanched of mauve glory & robbed
of their satin, a darkening edges
veined petals in stark relief, the buds
now fossils of their becoming.
I tend them as if freshly sheared from
the bush, as if their fragrance still sang
of spring. Beauty, bundled
to draw death out into a drawl, into
a dream you simply never wake from.
Dying lovely on my table, their heads
unbowed even as their stems soften
& turn nightshade in the water I change
daily, lavishing the care I don't have time for,
rinsing their rot from my fingers.
Whether I ever hear them or not,
their elegantly withered bodies blare
in the afternoon light, *grace is always grace!*

# THE SPIDER'S LESSON

Angel-friends have fed & loved me loud again,
listened & laughed with me until something inside
rose. We were coming back from a night of word-song
& dancing, of sweat & music begging the body
to move before it's too late when

eight legs, aglow in the streetlight,
crawled up & across the dashboard. I crazy-eighted
down the street, swerving wildly
from its proud creep. *Don't kill it! They're good luck!*
missed my ears as I smacked the spider senseless—
I've never been tender with my terrors, allowed them
to approach me first. I parked, leaving the crucified body
to pass away.

At 8 a.m., the sun & I crashed into the driver's seat.
It was the first morning I'd seen in months, every
sight/sound/smell crisp as the first day
of kindergarten. I was astonished at the web
glistening above the corpse-free dashboard,
the intricate beauty spun after the close call.

I crossed bridges & chased rivers home, trying to contain
my envy, suspicious of every itch, tingle.
Undaunted, it got me anyway, the spider's lesson
flaming my calf. I rubbed aloe into the proof—
thankful for each tiny resuscitation,
even the ones that bite.

# SPRING

Missing what's been lost
to all of the storms—
there's solace, as always,
by looking up.

The dogwood tree split
like a tuning fork
by Sandy's ravenous mouth—
stripped & rickety
all winter, blooming!

White petals adorn
the scarred body, flock
broken branches like leis
around necks in paradise,
lap at halved cambium & heartwood
like silk tongues, grooming.

I can't deny
such rapture anyway
or my own
as a pure note vibrates
here & now.

# TO A DEAR FRIEND MOTHERING MISERY

Every time your grief cries,
you pick it up, cradle it
like a newborn. But your pain
isn't precious, not your life-long
responsibility. For each doting moment,

your soul refuses to sing for days—& the world
needs your music too much.

Please leave it be; no more milk. Let it cry
for nights on end unattended. Let it
forget how your heartbeat sounds, the warmth
of your skin. Stop making it soup when it coughs,
setting a place for it at the table or buying it
new clothes. Convert its old room into
a sanctuary for things you adore.

Let your ache become self-sufficient
& grow apart from you,

walk out the door
& forget to call home.

# WHAT A SNAKEHEAD DISCOVERED IN A MARYLAND POND & A POET IN CORPORATE AMERICA HAVE IN COMMON

*The snakehead is a voracious fish from China's Yangtze River. It can breathe air and "walk" on land—able to crawl out of the water and survive for up to three days while searching for a new body of water if necessary. These critters could devastate the native ecosystem and be almost impossible to control.*

My fins are foreign, my gills versatile
because they've always had to be.
Despite alleged aggression,
I cut these teeth for protection.

You understand how the others swim,
but me—my travel mystifies,
terrifies a little.

You figure if you don't "get" me,
I'll somehow get you good—
invading & transforming the habitat forever.

*How do you do what you do?*
*Where are you coming from?*
*How should I manage you?*

I propelled myself upon rugged land
to reach this pond,
buried in the muddy bottom for years.

Both of us marvel
that I've survived this long undetected.
Keep your poisons, your devious nets, whatever
ridding you have in mind.

There is no need to slice & bleed me.
Just because I can, doesn't mean I ever planned
to wipe you out.

I've heaved my greatness before.
I'll do it again,
back to incredible, exotic waters in which
you would drown.

# VOYEUR

Watch how a struck river
composes itself after
each stone, rain.

Watch the water noose
then let loose
what it reflects.

Watch me become
woman as river
& run, run, run!

# LOVE LITANY

For Aracelis and Rassan, 8.3.13

Beloveds
What these two have is
a prime, stellar love
Intergalatic satellite
travellintravellintravellin
& lay next to me love
Starshine & Clay
come what may love
Accordion love
Exquisitely strung, fretless
strum by heart
music between our fingers love
Break it down, breakthrough
unbreakable love
Ripe blueberry love
Winged, humming love
Wherever we are love
Wherever we're going love
Increíble si amor
voilà, ici, toujours amour
Te Haguse, Tsebuk Fikré
Doux-doux darlin' love
Say it plain, let me explain love
Back in the day, yes we can
stand the rain & walk
right up to the sun love
Lay your head on my pillow
let me plant you a willow
knit you a sweater
write you a love letter love
Hello, it WAS me you were looking for love

Bedrock, take stock love
Deep sea diver, whale of a love
Sail through this to that love
All I wanna do, easy because
it's you love
So worth it, love is for everybody love
Dawn after dawn
dreamy, dusky love
Mo' betta, go-getter,
Thrilled & grateful
we know better love
Hold it now . . . hit it
& never quit it love
Until the trees & seas just up & fly away
Until the day that 8x8x8 is 4 love
Where have you been
yet right on time somehow love
Gourd full of earth, private harmony
heart shepherd kind of love
Altar in the sky
My Girmay goes with your Salandy love

# NOVEMBER MORNING PRAYER

The red maple leaf
through the barred window
blazes my eye
open, a bright thank you
on its dying lips.

So much goodness awaits;
icy skies cut-glass clear
above our heads, the meal
that will surprise our tongues
as we begin to know each other
over brunch in Brooklyn.

May whatever we discover
drip french-toast-doused-
in-maple-butter-syrup sweet.
May the short burst
of afternoon light
flood us with wonder
long past twilight's
periwinkle dream,

day & night slow-dragging
as old lovers remembering
the first time, the sun burning
opposite the complacent moon
until she ignites.

# WHAT IS BELIEVED IN IS TRUE

Nothing like a hoax at all, a text message
lights up the middle of my night
like a digital firefly: *Your father & I*
*are on the porch watching Mars*
*peek around the moon; its red eye*
*stares back. This won't happen again*
*until long after we are gone.* Okay, she didn't type it
exactly like that, but this is a faithful translation
by her daughter, a poet alone in a dark room

save for the now-open laptop screen & desire
for a recently magnified beauty rising
through dreams like the steam of some sacred bayou
or hot spring, awake from what beckons
with its distant red glow, a planet of pleasure
spinning close to my disrobed eye
yet orbiting just out of reach. Whether this glimmer
of something otherworldly in this woman's eyes
& laugh is simply meant to be seen, felt & admired,
or I gather glory fashioned from stardust
in my hands, lay in lush valleys & unleash rivers, I say thank you
to the cosmos—its apparitions & swirls of mystery
that suddenly become evident. I say amen & thank you
for the love I come from—a love that envisioned itself
into reality through a science of their own over 40 years ago.

Standing together so far away from me these days,
they measure themselves in relation to moons past,
gazing toward where beloveds
eventually travel with starry-eyed wonder.

# CASSANDRA

Grand Canyon voice
echoing across centuries
I leaned forward as far as I could
Fearless of falling in

Contralto siren
whose lips grazed the mic like
a kiss on the collarbone
Birthed lava tones that spread
through the melting crowd

Octopus voice
Touching everywhere at once
Light enough to ride
May's sweet evening breath
Deep enough to ease that low
throbbing pain
like Grandma humming Mahalia

Honey loc'ed songbird
Copper curves
embraced by burgundy silk
Moved thousands with a moan
The bassdrumguitar lacing
a hammock of sound
for her voice to recline in

She hop-scotched
Mississippi mud rhythms
Bellowed notes from reddened fields
Made old lovers remember
the salt of each other's skin

She turned us
into magnolias parting for rain

# STACY

is short for ecstasy spilling from sax,
from lips singed by smooth brown fire
cooling in a glass nearby, neat.
In the upper register, you turn angel
with large, copper Jesus hands.
Master of ringed breath, mouth
married to reed & rhythm, when we
hear you, we remember that angels
are almost always men. With bowed head,
eternal notes halo the room, at once
prophetic & profane as snakes, charmed
measures rise & sway, swoon. Ear pearls,
mercy blowing mistakes into miracles.
Dapper in jeans or suits, you endeavor
to recreate a woman's midnight
croon, to sound *at least* that free.
How does an instrument so light, leverage
legacies of skin, smoke, & salvation?
Blend thunder & sunshine, controlling
the weather of souls? Well, he's man enough
to conjure & support life in the brass womb,
songs tethered to him by black cord,
umbilical blues & reds feeding us intros
& outros, hellos & so longs.
On some nights, his body is a sail
& his horn ships us anywhere,
everywhere on rivers of this brother's love
undamned through music

# DAY AT THE DUNES

*I was conceived in these dunes, right here,*
our guide Rob says, touching the inked shack
on his arm, then pointing tanned muscles
out of the Expedition's driver-side window to the real one.
*Mom, too much information!* He teased,
but the pride is tattooed in his eyes. He is
Prince of the Dunes, because his father was Art,
King of the Dunes. Or should we say Pharaoh
for this stretch of Giza in New England, Race Point
treasure after deforestation, incredible proof of sweet yield
after erosion. Perhaps more like Moses, also led
by passion rather than profit, a life spent
escorting countless souls, tours offering a glimpse
of the eternal—as close as we can get until crossing.
I believe that any of these bushes could ignite
into prophesy right now, the beach plums we roll
in our hands & the basil we press to our noses
simple, deep revelations. My feet & the sand
one color, I gather sun-warmed handfuls,
leaving bits of myself behind forever. I wonder if
Tennessee Williams, Annie Dillard, & Jack Kerouac
felt at once ancient & infant as I do,
combing fine green hairs in the earth's shifting scalp,
perfect, slender hopes trembling. The scrapbook
holds pictures of more writers, presidents, stars, strangers,
& townies, recalls vows & ashes faithfully flung
into this same swift wind, & my brow, cheeks, & chin
lean into the sting & salve of recognition.
Ron ferries five women with him on the prodigious climb
of steel up soft slopes. Four of them are friends, two couples,
all of us connoisseurs of curves that give as they maintain shape.

We know what it means to exist as forgiving landscapes, each of us
fleeting dunes of flesh, especially Patience,
laughing louder than the whir of her oxygen machine,
gasping in awe when the white-tailed hawk swoops down,
yards away. We talk of those who've come & gone,
who dared to spend months, years, not just an hour,
this precious hour, & we think they knew more,
maybe even cared more. *They were made*
*of stronger stuff than us*, Patience sighs,
as our prince regaled us with encyclopedic facts, history,
& human tales gratifying as well-water,
or full of salt like the old man in the shack we passed
on the way out, his rusted bike chained to a driftwood post.
Maybe feeling so necessary & so superfluous
in the same breath devastated him, & he never recovered.

Clearly only spirit lasts out here, yet nineteen shacks
stubborn against the horizon. Some of us need
to build anyway—not just visit but live out closest
to the ominous, beautiful truth of it all.

# CATSKILLS RETREAT

On a mountain all moonglow
toad moan & green majesty,
I've come (since it wouldn't come to me)
to make peace at the foot of heaven,
haul it home somehow. The steepness
of my soul overwhelms housed
in this bear of a body.

Prophets prove that mountains midwife
great reckoning; the heart's
red psalms in concert
with the hummingbird's whirring,
thoughts linger awhile, embraced
by the naked mind. God-flecked
cypress & pine, I can't stand tall
with you—knees too burdened
to hike trails & dash meadows,
I am fat with failure & promise—
a pile of damp timber just before sunrise.

I take cool, high-altitude breaths
& recall other heights, gaze
at humbling shoulders of earth
brushing up against brazen blue—
channel a lily pad lightness upon
woman-made depths to face matters
long past skimming.

As fingers press prayers into
crumbling quartz, bless
my fellow travelers & the blades

of grass forgiving our steps, springing
back up. Bless the beaver beginning
again & again, the monarch's
meandering flight. Bless these mosquitoes
& their insatiable thirst, the bluejays
at dawn trilling *you are not through*

# NOTES

The collection's title is derived from Lucille Clifton's poem, "won't you celebrate with me," published in her collection, *Book of Light*.

In "Angel," the epigraph is from a *New York Times* article written by John Ligon, and the italicized line is a direct quote from Michael Brown, Jr. that was published in that article.

The poems "Hunt (1936 - )," "The Oak Tree's Burden," "For Jesse Washington," and "The Accused's Last Stand" were all written after viewing vintage postcards from the Without Sanctuary exhibit.

"Eternal Stand" is a sestina that breaks form when the flood waters enter the poem.

"Her Poem Stuns Mine Into Holding Its Head" uses a direct quote from a student that is italicized throughout the poem. The initial "L" is used in the epigraph for privacy.

"Song of Solomon Remix" uses five scenes from Toni Morrison's novel of the same name to fashion this poem.

The title, "Dear God Please Make Me a Bird, " is a line from the movie, *Forrest Gump*.

"A Golden Shovel" is a form that was created by Terrance Hayes that challenges poets to use a Gwendolyn Brooks poem or lines from one of her poems as the end words of new poems. There is an anthology edited by Peter Kahn and Ravi Shankar (University of Arkansas Press) that introduces the form and shares golden shovels by several esteemed writers. My golden shovel uses two lines from Brooks' poem, "A Sunset of the City."

The title "These Are the Breaks" references a popular rap song by Kurtis Blow. The italicized phrase "borrowed splendor" is from a poem by Rumi.

"Love Litany" includes several pop culture references and song lyrics throughout from Joni Mitchell, Bessie Smith, Lionel Richie, Stevie Wonder, The Isley Brothers, The Beastie Boys, and Minnie Riperton. Two lines are taken from Lucille Clifton poems: "Sail through this to that" and "Starshine and Clay."

## ACKNOWLEDGMENTS

Versions of these poems have appeared in the following journals &
anthologies:

*The Awl, Black Renaissance Noire, Callaloo, The Colorado Review,
Connotations Press, Drunken Boat, Fjords Review, Gathering Ground,
Harvard Review, HIV Here and Now Project, The Golden Shovel, The
Lodestar Quarterly, Mead, Obsidian III, The Offing, Poem-A-Day, Prairie
Schooner, The Ringing Ear, The Rumpus, Sable, The Same, Superstition
Review, Tupelo Quarterly, Washington Square Review, Waxwing, The Wide
Shore*, and *Villanelles*.

Special thanks to the Center for Faith & Work, Rose O'Neill Literary
House, Cave Canem, & the poets who gathered at the Chesapeake Bay
for the support & resources to complete portions of this book.

Thanks to Martha Rhodes, Ryan Murphy, & the entire Four Way Books
staff for another book journey.

Adrian Matejka, Tracy K. Smith, & D.A. Powell, thank you.

Mirjam Applehoff, Lauren Cerand, David Flores, & Verlon C. Malone,
thank you.

Grateful for my always / all ways sistar circle during this period: Yolonda
Baker, Laure-Anne Bosselaar, LaShonda K. Barnett, Natalie Diaz,
Camille Dungy, Aracelis Girmay, Stacey Joy Graham, Candance L.
Greene, Rachel Eliza Griffiths, Ellen Hagan, Lindsey Horne, Naomi
Jackson, TJ Jarrett, Tayari Jones, Nina Angela Mercer, Tonia Poteat,
Brenda Shaughnessy, Samantha Thornhill, Carey Wallace, & many
others.

Kamilah Aisha Moon is a Pushcart Prize winner, Lambda Award finalist and a 2015 New American Poet who has received fellowships to Vermont Studio Center, Rose O'Neill Literary House, Hedgebrook, and Cave Canem. Her work has been featured widely, including in *Harvard Review*, *Poem-A-Day*, *Prairie Schooner* and elsewhere. Moon holds an MFA from Sarah Lawrence College and is an Assistant Professor of Poetry and Creative Writing at Agnes Scott College.

Publication of this book was made possible by grants and donations. We are also grateful to those individuals who participated in our 2016 Build a Book Program. They are:

Anonymous (8), Evan Archer, Sally Ball, Jan Bender-Zanoni, Zeke Berman, Kristina Bicher, Carol Blum, Lee Briccetti, Deirdre Brill, Anthony Cappo, Carla & Steven Carlson, Maxwell Dana, Machi Davis, Monica Ferrell, Martha Webster & Robert Fuentes, Dorothy Goldman, Lauri Grossman, Steven Haas, Mary Heilner, Henry Israeli, Christopher Kempf, David Lee, Jen Levitt, Howard Levy, Owen Lewis, Paul Lisicky, Katie Longofono, Cynthia Lowen, Louise Mathias, Nathan McClain, Gregory McDonald, Britt Melewski, Kamilah Aisha Moon, Carolyn Murdoch, Tracey Orick, Zachary Pace, Gregory Pardlo, Allyson Paty, Marcia & Chris Pelletiere, Eileen Pollack, Barbara Preminger, Kevin Prufer, Peter & Jill Schireson, Roni & Richard Schotter, Soraya Shalforoosh, Peggy Shinner, James Snyder & Krista Fragos, Megan Staffel, Marjorie & Lew Tesser, Susan Walton, Calvin Wei, Abigail Wender, Allison Benis White, and Monica Youn.